I0817025

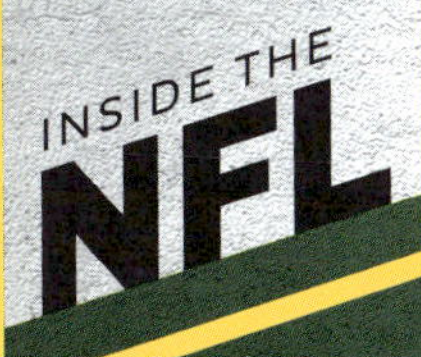

GREEN BAY PACKERS

BY TONY HUNTER

SportsZone
An Imprint of Abdo Publishing
abdobooks.com

abdobooks.com

Printed in the United States of America, North Mankato, Minnesota
042019
092019

Cover Photo: Jeff Haynes/Panini/AP Images
Interior Photos: Rob Tringali/SportsChrome/Getty Images, 5; Joe Robbins/Getty Images Sport/Getty Images, 7; Kevin Terrell/AP Images, 9; Pro Football Hall of Fame/AP Images, 11; AP Images, 13, 17, 23, 43; Bettmann/Getty Images, 14; NFL Photos/AP Images, 19, 27; Vernon Biever/AP Images, 21; Focus on Sport/Getty Images Sport/Getty Images, 25; Jay Dickman/Getty Images Sport/Getty Images, 29; David Stluka/AP Images, 30, 38; Doug Mills/AP Images, 33; Jay Drowns/Sporting News/Getty Images, 35; Mike Roemer/AP Images, 36; Morry Gash/AP Images, 40

Editor: Patrick Donnelly
Series Designer: Craig Hinton

Library of Congress Control Number: 2018965346

Publisher's Cataloging-in-Publication Data

Names: Hunter, Tony, author.
Title: Green Bay Packers / by Tony Hunter
Description: Minneapolis, Minnesota: Abdo Publishing, 2020 | Series: Inside the NFL | Includes online resources and index.
Identifiers: ISBN 9781532118470 (lib. bdg.) | ISBN 9781532172656 (ebook) | ISBN 9781644941065 (pbk.)
Subjects: LCSH: Green Bay Packers (Football team)--Juvenile literature. | National Football League--Juvenile literature. | Football teams--Juvenile literature. | American football--Juvenile literature.
Classification: DDC 796.33264--dc23

TABLE OF CONTENTS

CHAPTER 1

A RING FOR RODGERS

It is not easy to replace a legend. Winning a championship helps. That was the task Aaron Rodgers had in succeeding Brett Favre as quarterback of the Green Bay Packers.

Rodgers was a first-round draft pick in 2005. He was chosen to one day replace Favre. For three seasons, he waited as a backup. Then his turn finally came when the Packers made the surprising move to trade Favre in 2008.

Packers fans loved Favre and were not sure Rodgers could

SUCCESS AS A SIXTH SEED

The NFL playoff field expanded to six teams in each conference starting in 1990. Through the 2018 season, only two sixth-seeded teams had gone on to win the Super Bowl. The first was the Pittsburgh Steelers after the 2005 season. The Packers were the second, and the first NFC team to do so, five years later.

In the regular season, they went 10–6. They did not win their division. But their record was good enough to make the playoffs as a wild card. As the lowest seed in the National Football Conference (NFC) bracket, they would have to win three straight road games to reach the Super Bowl.

First the Packers traveled to Philadelphia to face the NFC East champion Eagles. Rodgers threw three touchdown passes as Green Bay held on for a 21–16 victory. Next up were the Atlanta Falcons, who had won the NFC South with a 13–3 record and were the NFC's top playoff seed. It wasn't even close. The Packers exploded for four touchdowns in the second quarter, silencing the fans at the Georgia Dome. Rodgers was brilliant, completing 31 of 36 passes for 366 yards and three touchdowns. The Packers cruised to a 48–21 victory.

That set up a trip to Chicago to face their biggest rivals in the NFC Championship Game. The Packers had split two games with the Bears that season. They lost a three-point

B. J. Raji, *left*, shakes off the tackle of Bears quarterback Caleb Hanie to score a touchdown in the NFC Championship Game.

heartbreaker at Soldier Field in September, then returned the favor with a 10–3 win in Green Bay in the season's final game. This time, a Super Bowl trip was on the line.

Rodgers and running back James Starks scored rushing touchdowns as the Packers took a 14–0 halftime lead. But the Bears scored early in the fourth quarter and got the ball back with a chance to tie the game. Then hulking defensive lineman B. J. Raji made the play of the game. He dropped back in pass

LUCKY 13

The Packers are one of the greatest teams in NFL history. The win in Super Bowl XLV gave them 13 NFL championships in their history. That was the most of any team. But most of those came before the Super Bowl era. Green Bay won nine NFL titles from 1929 to 1965. Then the Packers won Super Bowl titles after the 1966, 1967, 1996, and 2010 seasons.

coverage, where Bears quarterback Caleb Hanie wasn't expecting him to be. Raji stepped in front of Hanie's pass, made the interception, and rumbled 18 yards to the end zone for a touchdown. Green Bay held on to win 21–14.

The Packers faced the Pittsburgh Steelers in Super Bowl XLV. Rodgers bounced back from a shaky NFC Championship Game to have one of his best games as a pro. He completed 24 of 39 passes for 304 yards with three touchdowns and no interceptions, carving up a Steelers defense that was one of the best in the NFL. Rodgers completed just one of his first five passes, but he quickly heated up. He completed 10 of his next 11, including two touchdowns, as Packers built a 21–3 lead.

Pittsburgh closed the gap to 21–17 in the third quarter. But Rodgers hooked up with wide receiver Greg Jennings on an 8-yard touchdown pass early in the fourth quarter to put the Packers up 28–17. That was all the points they would need in a 31–25 victory.

Clay Matthews, *left*, and Aaron Rodgers celebrate after defeating the Steelers to win the Super Bowl.

Rodgers was named Super Bowl Most Valuable Player (MVP). Favre had won three league MVP awards but never one in the big game. He also had won only one Super Bowl title. Rodgers had matched him there. Rodgers was well on his way to winning over Green Bay's fans.

CHAPTER 2

EARLY SUCCESSES

Back in 1919, George Calhoun was a sports editor at the *Press-Gazette* in Green Bay, Wisconsin, who had a dream. Curly Lambeau was a former standout athlete from the area who shared Calhoun's vision. When the two men combined forces, something remarkable happened. That something was the creation of the Green Bay Packers.

Calhoun and Lambeau had crossed paths before. Lambeau was a star athlete at Green Bay East High School, and Calhoun had covered his games.

When they met up in 1919, they talked about starting up a football team. On August 11, 1919, a group of would-be players met at the newspaper's offices. From this meeting, a legendary NFL team was formed.

Curly Lambeau was a key figure in the Packers organization from 1919 to 1949.

JOHNNY "BLOOD" MCNALLY

Star halfback Johnny "Blood" McNally played for the Packers from 1929 through 1933 and then again from 1935 to 1936. McNally was a native of New Richmond, Wisconsin. He was a member of four NFL championship teams with the Packers. McNally was known for his speed, agility, and pass-catching ability. He was enshrined in the Pro Football Hall of Fame in 1963.

Lambeau worked for the Indian Packing Company. He convinced the owners to sponsor the team. They provided the $500 needed for a new set of blue and gold uniforms. The team also practiced on land owned by the company. In return for this sponsorship, the team was called the "Packers."

These humble origins were the start of a long, successful relationship between Lambeau and the Packers. Just 21 years old at the time, Lambeau took over as the team's player-coach for its first game against the Menominee North End A. C. in 1919. He went on to play halfback for 11 seasons and stayed on as the Packers' coach through the 1949 season.

The Packers were a dominant team from the start. In 1919 they went 10–1 against other teams that had formed in northern Michigan and Wisconsin. Their offense was a handful for opponents. They emphasized the passing game in an era when most teams preferred to run the ball.

Packers wide receiver Don Hutson was a two-time NFL MVP and a member of the Pro Football Hall of Fame All-1930s Team.

The Packers played home games at Hagemeister Park. It was located on the current site of Green Bay East High School. Instead of selling tickets, the Packers passed the hat at games, relying on fans' donations to help cover their expenses.

By 1921 the Acme Packing Company had bought the plant. Two of Acme's officials purchased the rights to own a team in

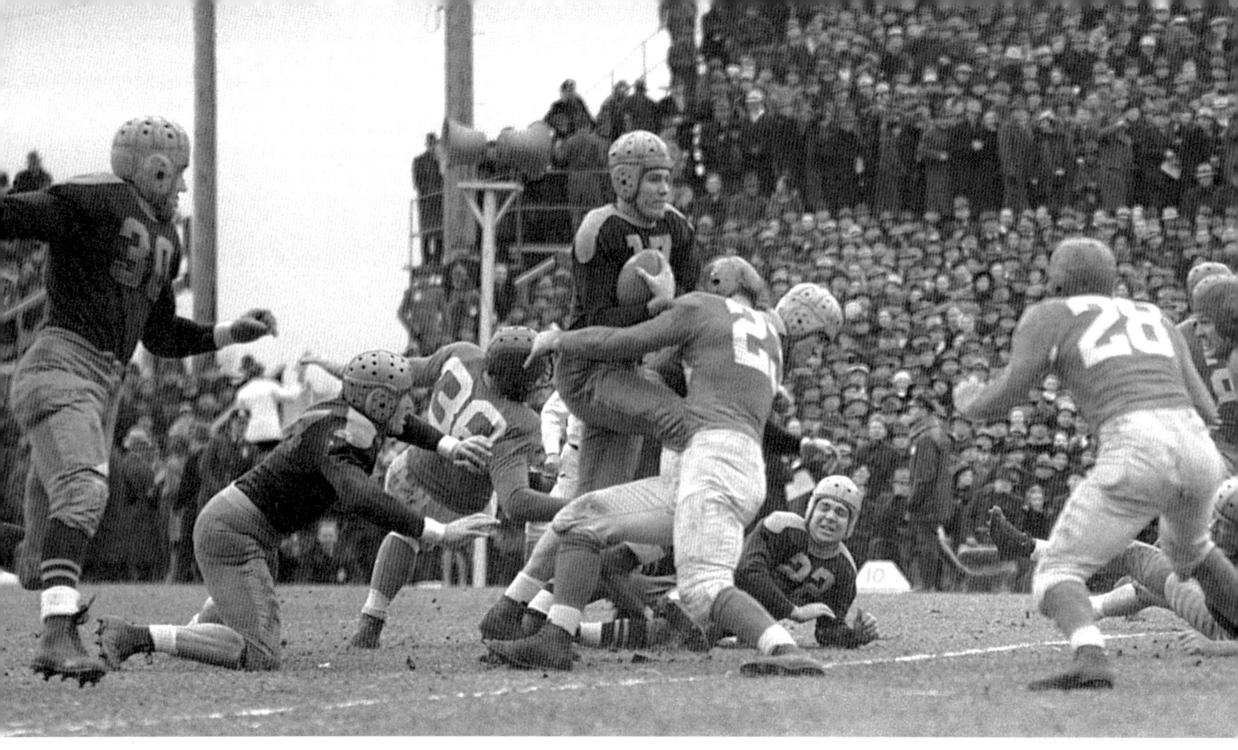

Cecil Isbell carries the ball against the Giants in the 1939 NFL Championship Game at State Fair Park in Milwaukee.

the American Professional Football Association (APFA), which would become the NFL a year later.

Calhoun served as the Packers' publicist, traveling secretary, and manager until 1947. He continued writing for the *Press-Gazette* as well. Andrew B. Turnbull, the newspaper's general manager, was the team's president from 1923 to 1928. He helped save the team after it struggled with financial problems.

In 1923 Turnbull devised a way to make the Packers a nonprofit corporation with shares of stock in the team owned by local businessmen at the time. That ownership structure remains in place today, making the Packers the only community-owned professional sports team.

It turned out to be a wildly successful move for Green Bay. Through the 2018 season, the Packers had won 13 league championships. The Chicago Bears ranked second with nine.

Green Bay won its first championship in 1929. The Packers outscored their opponents 198–22 and finished with a record of 12–0–1. At the time, the team that finished the season with the best winning percentage was declared the NFL champion.

The Packers were back on top in 1930. They went 10–3–1 for a .769 winning percentage, edging the New York Giants, who finished 13–4 (.765). Green Bay made it three titles in a row in 1931. The Packers went 12–2 and edged the Portsmouth Spartans (11–3) for the title. Green Bay's Johnny "Blood" McNally caught 11 touchdown passes that year.

The Packers came close to winning a fourth straight title in 1932. But back then, the NFL didn't count ties in the standings. Green Bay's 10–3–1 record was counted as 10 wins in 13 games (.769). The Bears finished 7–1–6, which counted as seven wins in eight games (.875). Under today's rules, with a tie counting as half a win and half a loss, the Packers' .750 winning percentage would have topped the Bears' .714 mark.

DON HUTSON

Roughly once a generation, a player comes along who revolutionizes a position. In the 1930s, that man was Don Hutson. Hutson was a dynamic wide receiver for the Packers from 1935 to 1945. He set 18 NFL receiving records in his career. Amazingly, considering how the modern passing game evolved, 10 of those records were still standing when Hutson died in 1997. Hutson also is often referred to as the NFL's first star wide receiver. As of 2018, among the NFL records he still held were most seasons leading the league in receptions (eight) and most seasons leading the league in receiving yards (seven).

The NFL began playing an official championship game after the 1933 season. The league split the teams into Eastern and Western divisions. Each division's winner earned a spot in the league title game.

In 1936 the Packers won the Western Division with a 10–1–1 record, earning their first berth in the NFL Championship Game. In the contest, Green Bay star wide receiver Don Hutson caught an early 48-yard touchdown pass from quarterback Arnie Herber. The Packers beat the Boston Redskins 21–6 at the Polo Grounds in New York.

In the 1939 NFL title game, the Packers beat the Giants 27–0 at State Fair Park in Milwaukee. Green Bay's sixth and final title under Lambeau came in 1944. Fullback Ted Fritsch scored two

The Packers celebrate their 1944 NFL title. Among those shown are fullback Ted Fritsch (64) and coach Curly Lambeau, *center*, in topcoat.

touchdowns—one rushing, one receiving—in the Packers' 14–7 win over the Giants at the Polo Grounds.

The Packers were successful even though they played in the NFL's smallest market. Even today, Green Bay's population barely tops 100,000. Operating without an owner, the Packers are one of the most unique stories in professional sports. More than 360,000 stockholders own some 5 million shares of the team.

The team and its fans had to endure some hard times in the 15 years after Lambeau's last title. But the 1960s would usher in a period of excellence unmatched in NFL history.

CHAPTER 3

THE LOMBARDI YEARS

The 1950s were a dreadful time for the Packers. Curly Lambeau had left to coach the Chicago Cardinals. The three coaches who followed Lambeau in Green Bay all had losing records. Between 1948 and 1958, the Packers did not have a winning season.

PAUL HORNUNG

Paul Hornung was a standout Packers running back in the late 1950s and 1960s. He won the Heisman Trophy, playing quarterback and safety at the University of Notre Dame in 1956. In 1957 the Packers chose Hornung first overall in the NFL Draft. Hornung played halfback and also was the Packers' field-goal kicker for several seasons. In 1960 he scored 176 points (15 touchdowns, 15 field goals, 41 extra points) to set an NFL record. In 1961 he was named league MVP. The NFL suspended Hornung and Detroit Lions star defensive tackle Alex Karras for the 1963 season for betting on league games. Both played again starting in 1964. Injuries forced Hornung to retire after the 1966 season.

Lombardi demanded discipline, focus, and, ultimately, perfection. He changed the Packers' attitudes.

Lombardi led the Packers to their first winning season in 12 years during the 1959 campaign. By 1960 Lombardi had guided Green Bay to the NFL Championship Game. The host Philadelphia Eagles beat the Packers 17–13. But Green Bay made amends the next year. The Packers defeated Lombardi's old Giants team 37–0 in Green Bay for the title.

In 1962 Green Bay went 13–1 and captured another NFL championship. The Packers toppled the host Giants 16–7 for the title.

Paul Hornung was a versatile star for the 1960s Packers.

After a two-year drought, the Packers won three straight NFL championships between 1965 and 1967. Included in that stretch were victories in the first two Super Bowls, after the 1966 and 1967 seasons. Today, the Super Bowl trophy is named after Lombardi.

From 1959 to 1967, Lombardi led Green Bay to five league championships. He compiled an 89–29–4 regular-season record and went 9–1 in the playoffs.

"He was the best coach ever, and I think few would question or argue that," said Jerry Kramer, a Packers guard from 1958 to 1968.

The Packers' star-studded roster helped Lombardi make the most of his efforts. One of the key cogs was offensive tackle Forrest Gregg. Gregg was named All-Pro eight times during his 14-season career in Green Bay, between 1956 and 1970. Lombardi once called him "the finest player I ever coached."

As of 2018, 12 players from the Lombardi era had been inducted into the Pro Football Hall of Fame. They include offensive linemen Kramer and Gregg, center Jim Ringo, quarterback Bart Starr, fullback Jim Taylor, running back Paul Hornung, defensive linemen Willie Davis and Henry Jordan, linebackers Ray Nitschke and Dave Robinson, cornerback Herb Adderley, and safety Willie Wood.

RAY NITSCHKE

Ray Nitschke was one of the most ferocious middle linebackers in NFL history. He played his entire career with the Packers, from 1958 to 1972. With a toothless, tough-guy look to him, Nitschke was dubbed "The Animal." It is doubtful that many creatures of the wild would have wanted to battle him. "He could put the fear of God into people," former Packers quarterback Bart Starr said. Nitschke was inducted into the Pro Football Hall of Fame in 1978.

Quarterback Bart Starr (15) sneaks in for the winning touchdown in Green Bay's 21–17 victory over Dallas in the "Ice Bowl."

Undoubtedly, the most memorable game of Lombardi's time with Green Bay came on December 31, 1967. That frigid day, the Packers defeated the visiting Dallas Cowboys 21–17 for the NFL title in a game later called "the Ice Bowl." The temperature at kickoff was minus-13 degrees Fahrenheit (minus-25°C). The windchill factor dipped to 36 degrees below zero (minus-38°C). Throughout the game at Lambeau Field, it only got colder.

The contest became one of the most unforgettable in league history. Starr scored from a yard out with just 13 seconds left to win the game. The touchdown gave the Packers their third straight NFL title. Two weeks later they defeated the

BART STARR

Bart Starr did not have the height of Peyton Manning or the cannon arm of Brett Favre. But Starr's mind, discipline, and surrounding talent helped make him one of the great winning quarterbacks in NFL history. Starr was only a seventeenth-round draft choice out of the University of Alabama in 1956. But he helped lead Green Bay to five NFL championships between 1961 and 1967. He also was the winning quarterback in the first two Super Bowls. His five NFL titles were matched only by New England's Tom Brady. Starr went 9–1 in playoff games and 74–20–4 in the regular season. He was the NFL's MVP in 1966 and the MVP of Super Bowls I and II.

Oakland Raiders in Super Bowl II, Lombardi's last game as the Packers' head coach.

Things were not always perfect with Lombardi. He was known to be tough on his players. But years later, his players all realized that Lombardi made them better players and men.

"He altered my life dramatically, and for the better," said Bob Long, a Packers wide receiver from 1964 to 1967. "He changed my football life and my business life, and I learned a lot from him. I learned to be mentally disciplined. I learned that in business, everything needs to be done correctly."

Lombardi coached the Packers through the 1967 season. He then stepped down and focused entirely on his job as the team's general manager.

Coach Vince Lombardi gets a lift from guard Jerry Kramer after the Packers defeated the Raiders 33–14 in Super Bowl II.

In 1969 Lombardi decided to accept a new challenge as coach of the Washington Redskins. He turned the team around. The Redskins broke a string of 13 straight seasons without a winning record. But Lombardi was diagnosed with cancer in June 1970. The cancer spread quickly. Lombardi died on September 3, 1970, at the age of 57.

Lombardi left behind a remarkable legacy. He helped solidify Green Bay's image as "Titletown USA." That is the nickname given to the city because of the Packers' success.

CHAPTER 4

DARKNESS BEFORE DAWN

Championships had become a way of life in tiny Green Bay, Wisconsin. Under coaches Curly Lambeau and Vince Lombardi, the Packers won 11 NFL titles between the 1929 and 1967 seasons. Then the team suffered through a long period of poor play.

Between 1968 and 1991, Green Bay had just five winning seasons. Only two coaches in that time took the Packers to the playoffs. Only one won a postseason game.

Dan Devine coached the Packers from 1971 to 1974. He

DRYER
89

JAMES LOFTON

One of the bright spots for Green Bay in the late 1970s through the mid-1980s was the play of wide receiver James Lofton. Lofton had 50 or more catches in seven of his nine seasons with Green Bay and reached 1,000 receiving yards in five seasons. He finished his Packers career with 530 receptions for 9,656 yards (a record since broken by Donald Driver) and 49 touchdowns. The speedy and athletic Lofton was enshrined in the Pro Football Hall of Fame in 2003.

the Los Angeles Rams for aging quarterback John Hadl. Green Bay gave up five early-round draft picks to acquire Hadl. He played just a season and a half for the Packers and did not perform well.

Bart Starr could not duplicate his success as a player when he took over as the Packers' coach and general manager. Between 1975 and 1983, Green Bay went 52–76–3 under Starr. The Packers qualified for the playoffs just once, in 1982. They defeated the visiting St. Louis Cardinals 41–16 in a wild-card playoff game. But Green Bay lost 37–26 to the host Dallas Cowboys in the next round.

The Packers tried turning back the clock again in 1984 when Forrest Gregg replaced Starr as head coach. Gregg had been one of the best offensive linemen in team history. But his coaching tenure was as disastrous as Starr's. Gregg went just 25–37–1 in his four seasons as coach.

Running back Eddie Lee Ivery (40) slashes through the line in the Packers' 37–26 playoff loss to the Cowboys in January 1983.

Things got better—but only slightly—under Lindy Infante. He coached the team from 1988 to 1991. The Packers were 10–6 in a memorable 1989 campaign. Third-year quarterback Don Majkowski emerged with a standout season. Majkowski was nicknamed the "Majik Man." Second-year wide receiver Sterling Sharpe became Majkowski's go-to target.

The 1991 offseason was a major turning point for the Packers. First, the team named Ron Wolf general manager on November 27, 1991. Wolf had worked in the front offices of the Oakland/Los Angeles Raiders and New York Jets. Wolf then quickly fired Infante and replaced him with Mike Holmgren.

Quarterback Brett Favre looks downfield during the Packers' 24–23 win over the Bengals on September 20, 1992.

Holmgren had achieved great success as the San Francisco 49ers' offensive coordinator.

On February 10, 1992, Wolf made a trade with the Atlanta Falcons for quarterback Brett Favre. Favre was a 1991 second-round pick but was not getting much playing time in Atlanta. Wolf thought highly of Favre and had wanted to draft him a year earlier.

Favre put his stamp on the hearts of Green Bay fans everywhere on September 20, 1992. He had replaced the injured Majkowski earlier in the game. The Packers trailed the visiting Cincinnati Bengals 23–17 with 19 seconds left. Green Bay was out of timeouts and 35 yards from the end zone.

The Packers called a play named "All Go." Favre threw a deep pass down the right sideline. The ball somehow split a pair of defenders and was caught by wide receiver Kitrick Taylor for a touchdown. The play gave the Packers an improbable 24–23 win.

Favre started the next game. He never left the lineup again during his 16 seasons in Green Bay. Together with Holmgren and Wolf, the Packers began a new era of dominance.

Another factor was the onset of free agency. Starting on March 1, 1993, players whose contracts expired were allowed to sign with any team. Before, a player's rights were owned indefinitely by the team that drafted him. The Packers used free agency to sign star defensive end Reggie White from the Philadelphia Eagles.

The Packers started winning in a big way. Holmgren led Green Bay to the postseason during his second and third seasons. Then, the 1995 Packers reached the NFC Championship Game. By the start of the 1996 season, the Packers expected a Super Bowl run. They delivered.

BRETT FAVRE

It is hard to imagine a time when Brett Favre was not one of the best quarterbacks in the NFL. But in his rookie season in Atlanta, Favre had few fans. Falcons coach Jerry Glanville once said it would take a plane crash for him to put Favre in a game.

But Ron Wolf saw something in Favre that inspired him to make the trade. And once Favre got in a game, he never left. Favre started an NFL- record 297 games in a row from 1992 to 2010. He played with Green Bay through the 2007 season.

When Favre was traded from Green Bay during the summer of 2008, he left with almost every passing record in team history. Among the categories in which Favre ranks first are touchdown passes (442) and passing yards (61,655). Favre was also the first player in NFL history to win three consecutive NFL MVP Awards. He was named to nine Pro Bowls as a Packer. He was a first- or second-team All-Pro selection five times.

Green Bay ranked first in the NFL in total offense and total defense in 1996. The Packers went 13–3 and dominated their opponents by a combined score of 456–210.

The Packers hosted and defeated San Francisco and the Carolina Panthers in the playoffs by a total score of 65–27 to reach Super Bowl XXXI. They faced the New England Patriots on January 26, 1997, at the Superdome in New Orleans.

Favre threw for 246 yards and two touchdowns with no interceptions. One of the touchdowns went for 81 yards to wide receiver Antonio Freeman. The other was a 54-yard strike

Brett Favre celebrates during Super Bowl XXXI in January 1997.

to fellow wideout Andre Rison. Favre also ran for a 2-yard touchdown. White also had a big game with three sacks.

Green Bay led 27–21 in the third quarter. Then Desmond Howard returned a kickoff 99 yards for a touchdown. The score gave the Packers some welcome breathing room. Green Bay held on to win 35–21, and the celebration began. The Packers had won their first NFL title in 29 years. But that did not mean they were satisfied.

CHAPTER 5

RETURN TO GLORY

Green Bay went back to the big game again the next season. In January 1998 the Packers traveled to San Diego as heavy favorites over the Denver Broncos in the Super Bowl. However, the Broncos and star quarterback John Elway upset the Packers 31–24. Terrell Davis rushed for 157 yards and three touchdowns for Denver.

The following season was Mike Holmgren's last as Packers coach. General manager Ron Wolf retired after the 2000 season. But with Favre continuing to play at an MVP level, the Packers stayed among the NFL's top teams.

Green Bay reached the postseason six times between 2001 and 2009 and played in the 2007 NFC Championship Game. The Packers hosted the New York Giants in freezing

Brett Favre played his final game as a Packer in frigid conditions at Lambeau Field in January 2008.

72

Packers quarterback Aaron Rodgers picks up some yards on the ground in his first NFL start, against the Minnesota Vikings at Lambeau Field on September 8, 2008.

cold conditions at Lambeau Field. The temperature at kickoff was minus-1 degree Fahrenheit (minus-18°C). The Packers usually had an advantage playing in the cold. But this time, they lost 23–20 in overtime.

It turned out to be Favre's last game as a Packer. With Favre aging and 2005 first-round pick Aaron Rodgers sitting on the bench, general manager Ted Thompson decided it was time to make a change. He traded Favre away after the 2007 season.

It was an extremely unpopular decision with fans. Favre earned their devotion over the years as he started 275 games in a row (including the playoffs) as a Packer. More importantly, the Packers went 172–103 in those games. In Favre's 16 seasons with Green Bay, the Packers finished with a losing record just once.

But Rodgers began making a name for himself right away. In his first two seasons as the starter—2008 and 2009—Rodgers threw for nearly 8,500 yards and 58 touchdowns with just 20 interceptions. He also led the Packers to the 2009 postseason. In the wild-card round, Green Bay lost 51–45 in overtime to the

KEEP WAITING

Packers season tickets are famously hard to get. Lambeau Field has sold out every game since 1960. The only way to get tickets is for fans to place their name on the team's waiting list. As of 2018, that list had more than 133,000 names. Many parents choose to add their children's names to the list as soon as they are born. But only approximately 100 new people get tickets each year. That means most fans will never get their chance at Packers season tickets.

Packers linebacker Clay Matthews fights off two Cowboys linemen en route to the quarterback.

host Arizona Cardinals. The 96 combined points set an NFL playoff record.

Rodgers reached his first Pro Bowl in 2009. He ranked fourth in the NFL in passer rating and threw for 4,434 yards.

More importantly, he led Green Bay to an 11–5 record and a postseason appearance.

Said Green Bay coach Mike McCarthy, "Aaron Rodgers is a Pro Bowl quarterback, and that's the facts. Trust me, I fully understand the greatness of Brett Favre. . . . But this is the beginning of potentially another great career at quarterback here in Green Bay, and (fans) should embrace it."

Rodgers rewarded fan patience the next year as the Packers broke through to their first Super Bowl title since the 1997 season. In just three years as a starter, Rodgers had equaled the number of titles Favre won. And in winning Super Bowl MVP, he had one title that Favre had never won.

Rodgers earned his first league MVP Award the next season as Green Bay went 15–1. That was the best record in team history. But the Packers suffered a shocking upset loss to the Giants in their first playoff game.

The Packers won four straight NFC North titles from 2011 to 2014.

CLAY MATTHEWS

With a future Hall of Famer in Aaron Rodgers, the Packers offense gets a lot of attention. But linebacker Clay Matthews was one of the best defensive players in football. He made the Pro Bowl six times in his first 10 seasons. In 2017 Matthews became the Packers' all-time leader in sacks.

Matt LaFleur is all smiles while being introduced as the Packers' head coach on January 9, 2019.

But they couldn't make it back to the Super Bowl, even as Rodgers won another MVP in 2014. They made the NFC Championship Game that season against the Seattle Seahawks. The Packers had a 16–7 lead entering the fourth quarter but lost in overtime.

After losing another NFC Championship Game following the 2016 season, an even bigger disaster occurred in 2017. The Packers were 4–1 going into a game with the Minnesota

Vikings. Rodgers took a hit from linebacker Anthony Barr that broke his collarbone. Green Bay went on to lose eight of its last 11 games. The Packers missed the playoffs for the first time since Rodgers's first year as a starter.

The losing continued in 2018 as the team went 6–9–1, and McCarthy lost his job in December. The Packers hired 39-year-old Matt LaFleur to replace McCarthy starting in 2019. He was the team's youngest head coach since Curly Lambeau and was just four years older than Rodgers.

"I think there's an incredible amount of talent here," LaFleur said. "Obviously when you have a quarterback of the caliber of Aaron Rodgers, we're going to have high expectations."

Packers fans hoped LaFleur's background as an offensive coordinator would be a good fit with Rodgers and give the quarterback a shot at bringing the Lombardi Trophy back to Titletown again.

WHO'S THAT?

The Packers are fortunate to have had two of the best quarterbacks to ever play the game. They've rarely had to worry about that position since 1991. In 2013 Aaron Rodgers got hurt and missed six games. Backups Matt Flynn, Scott Tolzien, and Seneca Wallace each started at least one game filling in for him. That was more quarterbacks than had started for Green Bay in the previous 20 years.

TIMELINE

1919

The Packers are founded on August 11 during a meeting at the *Green Bay Press-Gazette* newspaper office.

1929

Green Bay posts a 12–0–1 record and captures the first of three straight NFL titles.

1936

The Packers win their fourth NFL title with a 21–6 victory over Boston on December 13.

1959

On January 28, Vince Lombardi is named the Packers' head coach and general manager.

1961

The Packers win their first of five NFL titles in a seven-year span with a 37–0 home win over the Giants on December 31.

1967

Max McGee's seven catches for 138 yards and two touchdowns help Green Bay rout the Kansas City Chiefs 35–10 in Super Bowl I on January 15.

1967

On December 31, the Packers edge the Dallas Cowboys 21–17 in an NFL title game matchup that became known as "the Ice Bowl."

1968

Bart Starr completes 13 of 24 passes for 202 yards and a touchdown as the Packers defeat the Oakland Raiders 33–14 in Super Bowl II on January 14.

1992

On February 10, Packers general manager Ron Wolf trades a first-round draft pick to the Atlanta Falcons for quarterback Brett Favre.

1992

Favre throws two fourth-quarter touchdown passes to rally the Packers past the Cincinnati Bengals 24–23 on September 20.

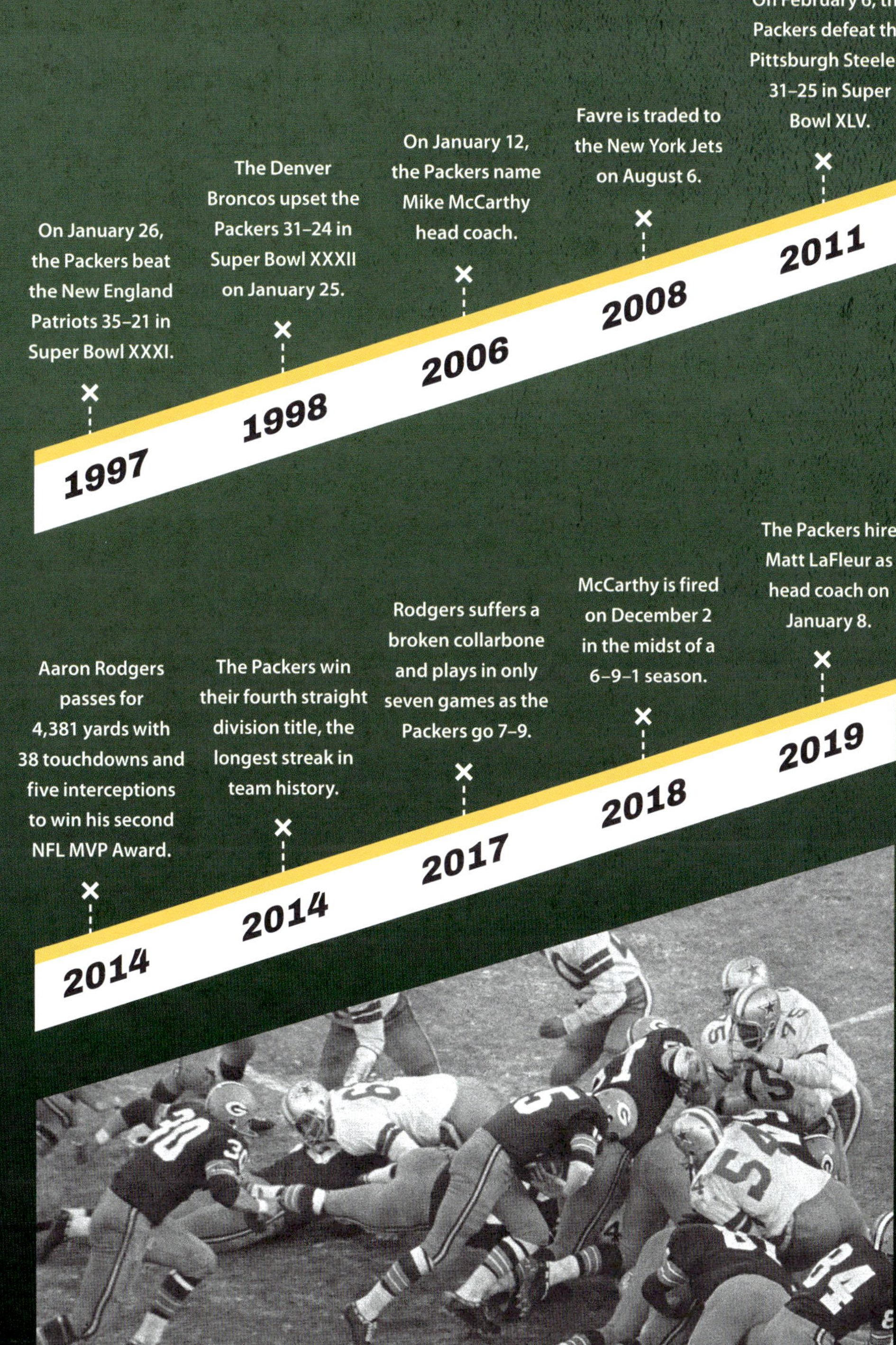

1997
On January 26, the Packers beat the New England Patriots 35–21 in Super Bowl XXXI.

1998
The Denver Broncos upset the Packers 31–24 in Super Bowl XXXII on January 25.

2006
On January 12, the Packers name Mike McCarthy head coach.

2008
Favre is traded to the New York Jets on August 6.

2011
On February 6, the Packers defeat the Pittsburgh Steelers 31–25 in Super Bowl XLV.

2014
Aaron Rodgers passes for 4,381 yards with 38 touchdowns and five interceptions to win his second NFL MVP Award.

2014
The Packers win their fourth straight division title, the longest streak in team history.

2017
Rodgers suffers a broken collarbone and plays in only seven games as the Packers go 7–9.

2018
McCarthy is fired on December 2 in the midst of a 6–9–1 season.

2019
The Packers hire Matt LaFleur as head coach on January 8.

QUICK STATS

FRANCHISE HISTORY

1921–

SUPER BOWLS *(wins in bold)*

1966 (I), **1967 (II)**, **1996 (XXXI)**, 1997 (XXXII), **2010 (XLV)**

NFL CHAMPIONSHIP GAMES *(wins in bold)*

1936, 1938, **1939**, **1944**, 1960, **1961**, **1962**, **1965**, **1966**, **1967**

NFC CHAMPIONSHIP GAMES *(since 1970 AFL-NFL merger)*

1995, 1996, 1997, 2007, 2010, 2014, 2016

KEY COACHES

Mike Holmgren (1992–98):
75–37, 9–5 (playoffs)
Earl (Curly) Lambeau (1921–49):
209–104–21, 3–2 (playoffs)
Vince Lombardi (1959–67):
89–29–4, 9–1 (playoffs)
Mike McCarthy (2006–18):
125–77–2, 10–8 (playoffs)

KEY PLAYERS *(position, seasons with team)*

Herb Adderley (CB, 1961–69)
LeRoy Butler (DB, 1990–2001)
Brett Favre (QB, 1992–2007)
Forrest Gregg (T, 1956, 1958–70)
Paul Hornung (RB, 1957–62, 1964–66)
Don Hutson (WR, 1935–45)
Clay Matthews (LB, 2009–)
Ray Nitschke (LB, 1958–72)
Aaron Rodgers (QB, 2005–)
Bart Starr (QB, 1956–71)
Jim Taylor (FB, 1958–66)
Reggie White (DE, 1993–98)
Willie Wood (DB, 1960–71)

HOME FIELDS *(in Green Bay)*

Lambeau Field (1957–)
Also known as
New City Stadium
City Stadium (1925–56)
Bellevue Field (1923–24)
Hagemeister Park (1921–22)

(in Milwaukee)

County Stadium (1953–94)
Marquette Stadium (1952)
Wisconsin State Fair Park (1934–51)

QUOTES AND ANECDOTES

"Maybe winning isn't everything, but it sure comes way ahead of whatever is second."

—Former Packers coach Vince Lombardi

For decades, the Packers played two or three regular-season home games each year in Milwaukee, Wisconsin. Most of those games were held at the State Fair Park fairgrounds and Milwaukee County Stadium. The Packers did not move their entire home schedule to Green Bay until 1995.

Until 2003 the Packers had never lost a home playoff game. They were 13–0, with 11 of the wins at Lambeau Field and two more in Milwaukee. The streak ended on January 4, 2003. The Atlanta Falcons defeated the Packers 27–7 in a wild-card game.

"Five letters here just for everybody out there in Packer-land: R-E-L-A-X . . . Relax. We're going to be OK."

—Packers quarterback Aaron Rodgers after fans were starting to panic when the team started 1–2 in 2014. Green Bay went on to finish 12–4 and made it to the NFC Championship Game.

GLOSSARY

contract
An agreement to play for a certain team.

draft
A system that allows teams to acquire new players coming into a league.

general manager
A team employee responsible for negotiating contracts with that team's players.

Hall of Fame
The highest honor a player or coach can get when his or her career is over.

postseason
Another word for playoffs; the time after the end of the regular season when teams play to determine a champion.

Pro Bowl
The NFL's all-star game, in which the best players in the league compete.

publicist
A person responsible for bringing positive attention to a product, person, or company.

retire
To end one's career.

rookie
A professional athlete in his or her first year of competition.

wild card
A team that makes the playoffs even though it did not win its division.

MORE INFORMATION

BOOKS

Graves, Will. *Best NFL Offenses of All Time*. Minneapolis, MN: Abdo Publishing, 2014.

Myers, Dan. *Green Bay Packers*. Minneapolis, MN: Abdo Publishing, 2017.

Trusdell, Brian. *The Most Dominant Dynasties of All Time*. Minneapolis, MN: Abdo Publishing, 2016.

ONLINE RESOURCES

To learn more about the Green Bay Packers, visit **abdobooklinks.com** or scan this QR code. These links are routinely monitored and updated to provide the most current information available.

PLACE TO VISIT

Lambeau Field
1265 Lombardi Ave.
Green Bay, WI 54304
920-569-7513
lambeaufield.com

This historic stadium, billed by the team as "the crown jewel of the NFL," opened in 1957 and most recently underwent a renovation that was completed in 2013. It also includes a team hall of fame that is open all year

INDEX

ABOUT THE AUTHOR

Tony Hunter is a writer from Castle Rock, Colorado. This is his first children's book series. He lives with his daughter and his trusty Rottweiler, Dan.